God's Con
New Beginnings

Satisfying, solid words of hope in times of change

Elim
Books
Come to the waters

www.ElimBooks.com

Selected by Kimberley Converse

God's Comfort Food for New Beginnings:
satisfying, solid words of hope in times of change
Copyright © 1999 by Kimberley Converse
All rights reserved.

Every effort has been made to find the original source for each quotation.
Contact the publisher with information about omissions or corrections.

Printed in 1999 in Canada; text printed on 100% recycled paper.

Elim Books, P.O. Box 704, Hampden, MA 01036
413.566.0282 voice   ~   413.566.2173 fax
www.ElimBooks.com   ~   Waters@ElimBooks.com

Inspiration/Self-Help
ISBN 1-893689-01-8

With my gratitude to

Dave Converse, Hannah Converse, Lauri Mikkola,
Sandra Decker, Rosalie Ferris,
Marlene Bagnull, Sharon Anderson,
Nan Lingenfelter, Denise Hackett,
Karen Duvall, Tricia Leal Welch, Barbara Robidoux,
Chris Young, Carol Munro, and Cindy Vlatas.

Each of these people encouraged me as we worked together
on <u>God's Comfort Food for New Beginnings</u>.
Thank you, thank you, thank you!

About the God's Comfort Food Series

Comfort foods are outwardly simple in their ingredients, in their preparation, and in their presentations. But comfort foods primarily feed our hearts and souls, rather than our bodies. Common foods such as a spoonful of real mashed potatoes or a dish of chocolate bread pudding or a bowl of soup with a thick slice of bread are comfort foods. These beckon us to sit down and to feast, to eat until we are satisfied.

The God's Comfort Food Series is outwardly simple in its elements, its preparation, and its format. God's comfort food is simply prepared, yet satisfying to the soul. Gentle quotes, familiar Bible verses, and homespun illustrations comprise God's Comfort Food. Through these God invites us to His banquet and "fills the hungry soul with goodness."
Psalm 107:9

"Comfort, whether human or divine, is pure and simple comfort."
Hannah Whitall Smith in <u>The God of All Comfort</u>

About the Selector

Kimberley Converse has a passion for God's Word, to apply it in her own life and then to express it clearly to others through writing. She is the coauthor of <u>The Myth of the Perfect Mother</u> and a contributing writer to <u>The Parents Resource Bible</u>. She also teaches women about motherhood, thriving through change, and career choices, as she speaks and consults.

Kimberley lives at The 1857 Farmhouse with her husband, her two children, and varying numbers of cats and chickens. She is involved in a small prayer/support group, a ministry to International students, her children's schools, and her community.

You can contact Kimberley by e-mailing Authors@ElimBooks.com

Introduction

*In pain is a new time born. These words from Adelbert Von Chamisso
tell us that new beginnings are not always of our own choosing. The
change that loss brings often necessitates beginning over. Whether the loss
has been dramatic or gradual, singular or multiple, we can be left
unsure of what to do next, even doubting if we want to begin again.
God sees our pain, knows our situation, and cares for us. His comfort
gives us the courage to begin again, the perseverance to keep at it, and the
hope to sustain us throughout the journey.*

*As you begin again, may this book of inspirational quotes give you
man's encouragement and God's hope to face the uncertainties of
new beginnings.*

Dedication

For Debbie
who had the courage,
in faith,
to begin again.

Never be afraid to trust
an unknown future
to a known God.
Corrie Ten Boom

"For I know the plans I have for you,"
declares the LORD, "plans to prosper you and not to harm you,
plans to give you hope and a future."
Jeremiah 29:11 NIV

Let us not look back in anger
or forward in fear,
but around in awareness.
James Thurber

'Do not anxiously look about you,
for I am your God.
I will strengthen you, surely I will help you.'
Isaiah 41:10 NASB

I simply can't build my hopes on a foundation
of confusion, misery and death ... I think...
peace and tranquillity will return again.
Anne Frank

As the whirlwind passeth, so is the wicked no more:
but the righteous is an everlasting foundation.
Proverbs 10:25 KJV

There's no disaster
that can't become a blessing.
Richard Bach

They will rebuild the ancient ruins and restore the places long devastated;
they will renew the ruined cities that have been devastated for generations.
Isaiah 61:4 NIV

The treatment the wound gets
determines whether time will bring
healing or hate.
Elsa McInnes

He heals the brokenhearted
and binds up their wounds.
Psalm 147:3 NIV

Restoration

The first four letters of the
word restoration spell rest,
which is where restoration begins.

Melinda Fish

*"Come to me, all you who are weary
and burdened, and I will give you rest."*
Matthew 11:28 NIV

Rest is not a matter of
doing absolutely nothing.
Rest is repair.
Daniel W. Josselyn

*The God of all grace, who has called you to
his eternal glory in Christ,
will himself restore, establish, and strengthen you.
1 Peter 5:10 RSV*

One word frees us of
all the weight and pain of life:
that word is love.
Sophocles

*"He will take great delight in you,
he will quiet you with his love,
he will rejoice over you with singing."*
Zephaniah 3:17 NIV

When love and skill work together,
expect a masterpiece.
John Ruskin

For we are God's workmanship,
created in Christ Jesus to do good works,
which God prepared in advance for us to do.
Ephesians 2:10 NIV

He who can implant courage
in the human soul
is the best physician.
Karl Von Knebel

"Be strong and courageous, and act;
do not fear nor be dismayed,
for the Lord God, my God, is with you."
1 Chronicles 28:20 NASB

The task ahead of us
is never as great
as the power behind us.
Ralph Waldo Emerson

My grace is sufficient for thee:
for my strength is made
perfect in weakness.
2 Corinthians 12:9 KJV

Gentleness

Nothing is so strong as gentleness,
and nothing is so gentle as true strength.
Ralph Sockman

*"A bruised reed he will not break,
and a smoldering wick he will not snuff out,
till he leads justice to victory."*
Matthew 12:20 NIV

The moment we recognize our complete
weakness... will be the very moment that
the Spirit of God will exhibit His power.

Oswald Chambers

*But we have this treasure in jars of clay
to show that this all-surpassing power is
from God and not from us.*
2 Corinthians 4:7 NIV

God doesn't always lighten our load,
sometimes he strengthens our backs.
Unknown

\\|/

Strengthen the feeble hands,
steady the knees that give way.
Isaiah 35:3 NIV

Whatever brings you to your knees in weakness carries the greatest potential for your personal success and spiritual victory.

Charles Stanley

Then Job arose, and rent his mantle, and shaved his head, and fell down upon the ground, and worshipped.
Job 1:20 KJV

You are never so strong
as when you forgive.
Kimberley Converse

———

Then said Jesus, Father, forgive them;
for they know not what they do.
Luke 23:34 KJV

We set a prisoner free and
then discover that the
prisoner we set free was us.

Lewis Smedes

*For if ye forgive men their trespasses,
your heavenly Father will also forgive you.*
Matthew 6:14 KJV

Never cut
what you can untie.
Joseph Joubert

*If it is possible, as far as it depends on you,
live at peace with everyone.
Romans 12:18 NIV*

No man is an island,
entire of itself.
John Donne

Confess your faults one to another,
and pray one for another,
that ye may be healed.
James 5:16 KJV

Heal the past;
live the present;
dream the future.
Unknown

This one thing I do,
forgetting those things which are behind, and
reaching forth unto those things which are before.
Philippians 3:13 KJV

He that lacks time to mourn,
lacks time to mend.
William Shakespeare

I was dumb and silent,
I refrained even from good;
and my sorrow grew worse.
Psalm 39:2 NASB

Tears

Give sorrow words:
the grief that does not speak whispers the o'er
fraught heart, and bids it break.

William Shakespeare

Blessed are they that mourn:
for they shall be comforted.
Matthew 5:4 KJV

My soul is a broken field,
plowed by pain.
Sara Teasdale

*The LORD is near to the brokenhearted,
and saves the crushed in spirit.
Psalm 34:18 RSV*

Compassion invites the honesty
that voices the unspeakable
and brings healing.
Susan Lenzkes

For he has not despised or disdained the suffering of the afflicted one;
he has not hidden his face from him
but has listened to his cry for help.
Psalm 22:24 NIV

Grief melts away
like snow in May.
George Herbert

Thou hast turned for me
my mourning into dancing.
Psalm 30:11 KJV

The past is a foreign country,
they do things differently there.
Unknown

You are no longer foreigners and aliens,
but fellow citizens with God's people.
Ephesians 2:19 NIV

We stand today
on the edge of a new frontier.
John F. Kennedy

Behold, I have set the land before you:
go in and possess the land
which the LORD sware unto your fathers.
Deuteronomy 1:8 KJV

Life

Live in today
because your past
is not your potential.
Unknown

"Do not call to mind the former things, Or ponder things of the past.
"Behold, I will do something new, Now it will spring forth;
Will you not be aware of it?"
Isaiah 43:18–19 NASB

We cannot put off living
until we are ready.
Jose Ortega Y Gasset

*Yet you do not know what your life
will be like tomorrow.*
James 4:14 NASB

We have nothing to fear
but fear itself.
Franklin Roosevelt

*For you have not received a spirit
of slavery leading to fear again,
but you have received a spirit of adoption as sons.*
Romans 8:15 NASB

This extraordinary change of life could only take place in the structure of the everyday—houses and gardens, marriages.

Eugene H. Peterson

'Build houses and live in them; and
plant gardens, and eat their produce.
'Take wives and become the fathers of sons and daughters.'
Jeremiah 29:5–6 NASB

Redeem the time.
T. S. Eliot

＼｜／

*And I will restore to you
the years that the locust hath eaten.
Joel 2:25 KJV*

Gratitude

And we rejoice
at the new life.
Amarillo Globe-News

*He put a new song in my mouth,
a song of praise to our God.
Psalm 40:3 NASB*

Those who wish to sing
always find a song.
Swedish Proverb

Sing to him a new song,
play skilfully on the strings,
with loud shouts.
Psalm 33:3 RSV

To awaken each morning with the
thoughts of praise and gratitude
prepares us for the blessing of the day.
Dr. Catherine M. Sanders

This is the day which the LORD hath made;
we will rejoice and be glad in it.
Psalm 118:24 KJV

A life in thankfulness
releases the glory of God.
Bengt Sundberg

*But thanks be to God, which
giveth us the victory through our Lord Jesus Christ.
1 Corinthians 15:57 KJV*

The greater the obstacle,
the more glory
in overcoming it.
Molière

"The glory of this present house will be
greater than the glory of the former house."
Haggai 2:9 NIV

Gratitude makes sense of our past,
brings peace for today,
and creates a vision for tomorrow.

Melody Beattie

*Since we receive a kingdom which
cannot be shaken, let us show gratitude.*
Hebrews 12:28 NASB

Vision

If we will but let our God and Father
work his will with us, there can be no limit
to his enlargement of our existence.

George Macdonald

*Enlarge the place of thy tent, and let them
stretch forth the curtains of thine habitations: spare not,
lengthen thy cords, and strengthen thy stakes.*

Isaiah 54:2 KJV

You see things and say, "Why?",
but I dream things and say, "Why not?"
George Bernard Shaw

Now faith is the substance of things hoped for,
the evidence of things not seen.
Hebrews 11:1 KJV

Dreams are
necessary to life.
Anaïs Nin

\\|/

*Desire realized is
sweet to the soul.*
Proverbs 13:19 NASB

To see things in the seed,
that is genius.
Lao-Tzu

*"The kingdom of heaven is like a mustard seed...
yet when it grows, it is the largest of garden plants."*
Matthew 13:31–32 NIV

You should look in
suffering for the seeds of
your future spiritual growth.
Leo Tolstoy

Keep your eyes on Jesus...
He was willing to die a shameful death on the cross
because of the joy he knew would be his afterwards.
Hebrews 12:2 TLB

We cannot become
what we need to be
by remaining what we are.
Max Depree

＼∣／

*"I have been crucified with Christ;
and it is no longer I who live,
but Christ lives in me."*
Galatians 2:20 NASB

Only a man who knows what it is like to be defeated
can reach down to the bottom of his soul and come up
with the extra ounce of power it takes to win.
Muhammad Ali

*We are afflicted in every way, but not crushed;
perplexed, but not despairing; persecuted, but not forsaken;
struck down, but not destroyed.*
2 Corinthians 4:8–9 NASB

Truth

People grow through experience
if they meet life honestly and courageously.
Eleanor Roosevelt

\\|/

But speaking the truth in love,
we are to grow up in all aspects into Him... Christ.
Ephesians 4:15 NASB

Truth, whether you perceive it or not,
only brings light into your life.
Oprah Winfrey

⟍⎮⟋

"Then you will know the truth,
and the truth will set you free."
John 8:32 NIV

Healing always takes place
in the light.

Henry Cloud and John Townsend

Behold, thou desirest truth in the inward parts:
and in the hidden part thou shalt make me to know wisdom.
Psalm 51:6 KJV

Don't be reckless with other people's hearts.
Don't put up with people who are
reckless with yours.

Kurt Vonnegut

Keep your heart with all vigilance;
for from it flow the springs of life.
Proverbs 4:23 RSV

Wisdom is nothing more
than healed pain.
Robert Gary Lee

Know also that wisdom is sweet to your soul;
if you find it, there is a future hope for you,
and your hope will not be cut off.
Proverbs 24:14 NIV

The future belongs
to those who believe
in the beauty of their dreams.
Lincoln Steffens

Strength and dignity are her clothing,
And she smiles at the future.
Proverbs 31:25 NASB

What we see depends mainly
on what we look for.
John Lubbock

Come and see the works of God,
Who is awesome in His deeds
toward the sons of men.
Psalm 66:5 NASB

Mind-set

Reflect on your present blessings,
of which every man has many, not on your past
misfortunes, of which all men have some.

Charles Dickens

*You'll do best by filling your minds and meditating on things
true, noble, reputable, authentic, compelling, gracious—
the best, not the worst.*

Philippians 4:8 TM

The most important of life's battles
is the one we fight daily in the
silent chambers of the soul.

David O. McKay

Thou wilt keep him in perfect peace,
whose mind is stayed on thee:
because he trusteth in thee.
Isaiah 26:3 KJV

It's a matter of
"mind over matter."
Kimberley Converse

---

*Do not be conformed to this world but be transformed by
the renewal of your mind, that you may prove what is the will of God,
what is good and acceptable and perfect.*
Romans 12:2 RSV

It's not the monuments
that teaches us history.
It's the ruins.
Carl Hammarén

We are destroying speculations and every lofty thing
raised up against the knowledge of God, and we are
taking every thought captive to the obedience of Christ.
2 Corinthians 10:5 NASB

The horror of the dark days
makes me love the light even more.
Patty Smith

\|/

He brought them out of darkness and the shadow of death,
and broke their bands apart.
Let them give thanks to the Lord for His lovingkindness.
Psalm 107:14–15 NASB

Our greatest glory is not in never failing
but in rising up every time we fail.
Ralph Waldo Emerson

\\\ | //

For a just man falleth seven times,
and riseth up again.
Proverbs 24:16 KJV

I fall so miserably
into the chasm of disbelief
that I cry out in despair.
Maya Angelou

In my anguish I cried to the LORD,
and He answered by setting me free.
Psalm 118:5 NIV

Every day is a fresh beginning.
Susan Coolidge

\|/

The Lord's lovingkindnesses indeed never cease,
For His compassions never fail.
They are new every morning.
Lamentations 3:22–23 NASB

Vitality shows in not only
the ability to persist
but the ability to start over.
F. Scott Fitzgerald

*For you were continually straying like sheep,
but now you have returned to the
Shepherd and Guardian of your souls.
1 Peter 2:25 NASB*

Grace fills empty space,
but it can only enter where
there is a void to receive it.
Simone Weil

*It is good for the heart to be strengthened
by grace, not by foods.*
Hebrews 13:9 NASB

To keep a lamp burning
we have to keep putting oil into it.
Mother Teresa

*Kindle afresh the gift of God
which is in you.*
2 Timothy 1:6 NASB

Every soul is a melody
which needs renewing.
Stephane Mallarme

＼｜／

But they that wait upon the LORD shall renew their strength;
they shall mount up with wings as eagles; they shall run,
and not be weary; and they shall walk, and not faint.
Isaiah 40:31 KJV

Hope

We must accept finite disappointment,
but we must never lose infinite hope.

Martin Luther King, Jr.

We also exult in our tribulations... and hope does not disappoint,
because the love of God has been poured out within
our hearts through the Holy Spirit.

Romans 5:3–5 NASB

He that lives in hope
danceth without musick.
George Herbert

Though the fig tree does not bud and there are no grapes on the vines,
though the olive crop fails and the fields produce no food...
yet I will rejoice in the LORD.
Habakkuk 3:17–18 NIV

Not everything that can be counted counts, and
not everything that counts can be counted.
Albert Einstein

"A man's life does not consist
in the abundance of his possessions."
Luke 12:15 NIV

Blues are the songs of despair,
but gospel songs are the songs of hope.
Mahalia Jackson

*I am overwhelmed with joy
despite all our troubles.
2 Corinthians 7:4 TM*

He who has a why to live
can bear almost any how.
Friedrich Nietzsche

---

*That I may know Him [Christ], and the power of His
resurrection and the fellowship of His sufferings,
being conformed to His death.*
Philippians 3:10 NASB

Like blooms through melting snow,
long awaited color returns to life.
Charles Swindoll

See! The winter is past...
Flowers appear on the earth.
Song of Songs 2:11–12 NIV

Growth is the only evidence of life.
Unknown

\\|//

But grow in the grace and knowledge
of our Lord and Savior Jesus Christ.
2 Peter 3:18 NIV

Love

God loves us the way we are
but He loves us too much
to leave us that way.
Leighton Ford

*By his great mercy we have been born anew to a living hope
through the resurrection of Jesus Christ from the dead, and
to an inheritance which is imperishable, undefiled, and unfading.*
1 Peter 1:3–4 RSV

To be brought into the zone of the call of God
is to be profoundly altered.
Oswald Chambers

But we all, with open face beholding as in a glass the glory of the Lord,
are changed into the same image from glory to glory,
even as by the Spirit of the Lord.
2 Corinthians 3:18 KJV

But before change can occur,
we must know what it is
that needs changing.
Unknown

"But when He, the Spirit of truth comes,
He will guide you into all the truth."
John 16:13 NASB

When all else fails,
read the instructions.
Agnes Allen

⁂

The law of the LORD is perfect,
restoring the soul.
Psalm 19:7 NASB

You change your life
by changing your heart.
Max Lucado

"I will give them an undivided heart and put a new spirit in them;
I will remove from them their heart of stone
and give them a heart of flesh."
Ezekiel 11:19 NIV

The main thing is to
keep the main thing the main thing.

Stephen R. Covey

But the goal of our instruction is love from a pure heart and
a good conscience and a sincere faith.
1 Timothy 1:5 NASB

What we love
we shall grow to resemble.
Bernard of Clairvaux

And we, who with unveiled faces all reflect the Lord's glory,
are being transformed into his likeness.
2 Corinthians 3:18 NIV

Freedom

We must be willing to get rid of
the life we've planned, so as to have
the life that is waiting for us.
Joseph Campbell

But whatever things were gain to me,
those things I have counted as loss
for the sake of Christ.
Philippians 3:7 NASB

He is no fool who
gives what he cannot keep
to gain what he cannot lose.
Jim Elliot

You have been born anew,
not of perishable seed but of imperishable,
through the living and abiding word of God.
1 Peter 1:23 RSV

Fear can hold you prisoner,
hope can set you free.
Unknown

\\|/

Come to the place of safety,
all you prisoners, for there is yet hope!
Zechariah 9:12 TLB

If you give up the need for security,
you will be secure.
Unknown

∖∣⁄

There is no fear in love;
but perfect love casteth out fear: because fear hath torment.
He that feareth is not made perfect in love.
1 John 4:18 KJV

When you blame others,
you give up your power to change.
Dr. Robert Anthony

\\\|//

But if ye do not forgive,
neither will your Father which is in heaven
forgive your trespasses.
Mark 11:26 KJV

Don't find fault,
find a remedy.
Henry Ford

\/|/

Blessed are the merciful:
for they shall obtain mercy.
Matthew 5:7 KJV

Better to light a candle
than to curse the darkness.
Chinese Proverb

For God who said, "Light shall shine out of darkness,"
is the One who has shone in our hearts to give the light
of the knowledge of the glory of God in the face of Christ.
2 Corinthians 4:6 NASB

We must learn to reawaken and
keep ourselves awake, not by mechanical aids,
but by an infinite expectation of the dawn.
Henry David Thoreau

*God will help her
when morning dawns.
Psalm 46:5 NASB*

A person starts to live
when he can live outside himself.
Albert Einstein

We can comfort those in any trouble
with the comfort we ourselves have received from God.
2 Corinthians 1:4 NIV

The highest reward for a person's toil
is not what they get for it,
but what they become by it.
John Ruskin

*I consider that our present sufferings are not worth
comparing with the glory that will be revealed in us.*
Romans 8:18 NIV

Safe Place

I don't know what the future holds,
but I know who holds the future.
E.S. Jones

He is before all things,
and in him all things hold together.
Colossians 1:17 RSV

There is never a safer place to be,
than in God's loving hands.

Unknown

———— \\|/ ————

"I will take hold of your hand.
I will keep you."
Isaiah 42:6 NIV

We need courage to throw away
the old garments which have had their day.
Fridtjof Nansen

\\ | /

You removed my sackcloth and
clothed me with joy, that my heart may sing.
Psalm 30:11–12 NIV

It's so strange that such beauty
can come from such horror.
Willem Jan Grootjans

To bestow on them a crown of beauty instead of ashes,
the oil of gladness instead of mourning,
and a garment of praise instead of a spirit of despair.
Isaiah 61:3 NIV

It's not what you were,
it's whose you are.
Kimberley Converse

\\ / /

Once you were not a people,
but now you are the people of God.
1 Peter 2:10 NIV

Never underestimate
the power of love.
Unknown

In all these things we are more than
conquerors through him that loved us.
Romans 8:37 KJV

Freedom means
choosing your burden.
Hephzibah Menuhin

*Though you were slaves of sin, you became obedient from the heart
to that form of teaching to which you were committed,
and having been freed from sin, you became slaves of righteousness.
Romans 6:17–18 NASB*

Perseverance

The ground of liberty
is to be gained in inches.
Thomas Jefferson

\\|/

Little by little I will drive them out from before you,
until you are increased and possess the land.
Exodus 23:30 RSV

No man is entitled to the blessings of freedom
unless he be vigilant in its preservation.
Douglas MacArthur

*It is for freedom that Christ has set us free.
Stand firm, then, and do not let yourselves be
burdened again by a yoke of slavery.
Galatians 5:1 NIV*

The best way out
is always through.
Robert Frost

\\|/

We went through fire and water,
but you brought us to a place of abundance.
Psalm 66:12 NIV

It was the triumph of
hope over experience.
Samuel Johnson

*But in all these things we overwhelmingly
conquer through Him who loved us.
Romans 8:37 NASB*

Overcoming

Your current safe boundaries
were once unknown frontiers.
Unknown

Now that faith has come,
we are no longer under the supervision of the law.
Galatians 3:25 NIV

Time alone has no power to heal—
God alone does.
Susan Lenzkes

\\|/

I am the LORD that healeth thee.
Exodus 15:26 KJV

Simply pushing harder within
the old boundaries will not do.
Karl Weick

\\ / /

We have been released from the Law,
having died to that by which we were bound,
so that we serve in newness of the Spirit and not in oldness of the letter.
Romans 7:6 NASB

Ah, but a man's reach
should exceed his grasp,
or what's a heaven for?
Robert Browning

*I do not regard myself as having laid hold of it yet;
but... I press on toward the goal for the prize
of the upward call of God in Christ Jesus.
Philippians 3:13–14 NASB*

Freedom lies in being bold.
Robert Frost

For God hath not given us the spirit of fear;
but of power, and of love, and of a sound mind.
2 Timothy 1:7 KJV

You may have to fight a battle
more than once to win it.
Margaret Thatcher

For you have need of endurance,
so that you may do the will of God and
receive what is promised.
Hebrews 10:36 RSV

Never confuse a single defeat
with a final victory.
F. Scott Fitzgerald

*This is the victory that overcometh the world,
even our faith.
1 John 5:4 KJV*

Difficulties are meant to rouse,
not discourage.
William Ellery Channing

\\|/

We glory in tribulations also:
knowing that tribulation worketh patience;
And patience, experience; and experience, hope.
Romans 5:3–4 KJV

Out of every crisis comes
the chance to be reborn.
Nena O'Neill

———— ＼＼｜／／ ————

Jesus said unto her, I am the resurrection, and the life:
he that believeth in me, though he were dead, yet shall he live.
John 11:25 KJV

Success consists of going
from failure to failure
without loss of enthusiasm.
Winston Churchill

You greatly rejoice, even though now for a little while,
if necessary, you have been distressed by various trials.
I Peter 1:6 NASB

Great works are performed
not by strength
but by perseverance.
Samuel Johnson

Blessed is a man who perseveres under trial;
for once he has been approved,
he will receive the crown of life.
James 1:12 NASB

Life is difficult.
M. Scott Peck

\\|/

Dear friends, do not be surprised
at the painful trial you are suffering,
as though something strange were happening to you.
1 Peter 4:12 NIV

All the world is full of suffering.
It is also full of overcoming it.
Helen Keller

*"In this world you will have trouble.
But take heart! I have overcome the world."*
John 16:33 NIV

Possibilities

Sometimes you must do
the thing you cannot do.
Eleanor Roosevelt

"Do not say, 'I am only a child.'
You must go to everyone I send you to and
say whatever I command you."
Jeremiah 1:7 NIV

Sow a habit, and you reap a character.
Sow a character, and you reap a destiny.
Charles Reade

\\|/

*The things you have learned and received and heard and seen in me,
practice these things, and the God of peace will be with you.
Philippians 4:9 NASB*

Whether you believe you can,
or whether you believe you can't,
you're absolutely right.
Henry Ford

For as he thinketh in his heart,
so is he.
Proverbs 23:7 KJV

Stop thinking in terms of limitations...
Terry Josephson

And they said to Him,
"We have here only five loaves and two fish."
Matthew 14:17 NASB

...and start thinking in terms of possibilities.
Terry Josephson

\\|/

I can do all things through
Christ which strengtheneth me.
Philippians 4:13 KJV

Well done is better
than well said.
Benjamin Franklin

For the kingdom of God is not in word,
but in power.
1 Corinthians 4:20 KJV

As is our confidence,
so is our capacity.
William Hazlitt

In quietness and confidence
is your strength.
Isaiah 30:15 TLB

Prayer is the secret work that
develops a life that is
thoroughly authentic and deeply human.
Eugene H. Peterson

*But thou, when thou prayest, enter into thy closet,
and when thou hast shut thy door, pray to thy Father which is in secret;
and thy Father which seeth in secret shall reward thee openly.
Matthew 6:6 KJV*

What happens to a man is less significant
than what happens within him.
Louis L. Mann

Therefore we do not lose heart, but though our outer man is decaying,
yet our inner man is being renewed day by day.
2 Corinthians 4:16 NASB

Him

It is impossible for that
man to despair who remembers that
his Helper is omnipotent.
Henry Ward Beecher

*For I know whom I have believed and
I am convinced that He is able
to guard what I have entrusted to Him until that day.
2 Timothy 1:12 NASB*

What does not kill me
makes me stronger.
Friedrich Nietzsche

\|/

"God has made me fruitful
in the land of my suffering."
Genesis 41:52 NIV

The difficult times pull us inward
and urge us to search for
our connectedness to a higher power.
Dr. Catherine M. Sanders

You let the distress bring you to God,
not drive you from him.
2 Corinthians 7:9 TM

The stronger the winds, the deeper the roots.
The deeper the roots and the longer the winds,
the more beautiful the tree.
Charles Swindoll

*And he shall be like a tree planted by the rivers of water,
that bringeth forth his fruit in his season; his leaf also shall not wither;
and whatsoever he doeth shall prosper.
Psalm 1:3 KJV*

Our real blessings often appear to us
in the shapes of pains, losses and disappointments;
but let us have patience.
Joseph Addison

———— \\|// ————

Perseverance must finish its work
so that you may be mature and complete,
not lacking anything.
James 1:4 NIV

We must learn that the setbacks and griefs which we endure help us in our marching onward.

Henry Ford

\\|/

I consider that the sufferings of this present time are not worth comparing with the glory that is to be revealed to us.

Romans 8:18 RSV

Renewal

We turn not older with years,
but newer every day.
Emily Dickinson

\\ | /

Put on the new self who is being renewed to a true knowledge
according to the image of the One who created him.
Colossians 3:10 NASB

We may not be what we want to be,
but thank God we are not
what we used to be.

Tim Storey

He brought me up also out of an horrible pit, out of the miry clay,
and set my feet upon a rock, and established my goings.
Psalm 40:2 KJV

We know what we are,
but know not what we may be.
William Shakespeare

Beloved, we are God's children now;
it does not yet appear what we shall be,
but we know that when he appears we shall be like him.
1 John 3:2 RSV

Dost thou love life?
Then do not squander time,
for that is the stuff life is made of.
Benjamin Franklin

So teach us to number our days,
That we may present to You a heart of wisdom.
Psalm 90:12 NASB

It is not length of life,
but depth of life.
Ralph Waldo Emerson

May you be able to feel and understand, as all God's children should,
how long, how wide, how deep, and how high his love really is;
and to experience this love for yourselves.
Ephesians 3:18–19 TLB

Earth has no sorrow
that heaven cannot heal.

Thomas Moore

\\|/

They will enter Zion with singing; everlasting joy will crown their heads.
Gladness and joy will overtake them, and
sorrow and sighing will flee away.
Isaiah 35:10 NIV

And like any ending,
it was also a beginning.
Robin Schafer

*See, the former things have taken place,
and new things I declare.
Isaiah 42:9 NIV*

About Elim Books

Years ago I read the account of how the nation of Israel was set free after four hundred years of slavery. They passed through the Red Sea; wandered in the desert; stayed at Marah, which is a place that had bitter water; and wandered in the desert again. Discouraged, tired, and weary, "Then they came to Elim where there were twelve springs and seventy date palms" (Exodus 15:27). God had provided a place for them to be refreshed (water), nourished (date palms), and enkindled (given heart to continue the journey). Elim was a place where they began to heal. Based on what Elim meant, it fit what I wanted to do in a publishing company —
refresh, nourish, and enkindle journeying souls.
Kimberley Converse, Publisher

Elim
Books

P.O. Box 704 ~ Hampden, MA 01036
413.566.0282 voice ~ 413.566.2173 fax
~ www.ElimBooks.com ~
~ Waters@ElimBooks.com ~